THE DOORWAY

and other poems

R.K. PAVIA

The Doorway – and other poems

Published by Mage Guild Publishing in 2016
First Edition

Cover design by SelfPubBookCovers.com/Mystic
e-book formatting by Jim Proctor

A CIP catalogue record for this book is available from the British Library.
ISBN: 0992751675
ISBN-13: 978-0992751678

For my children.

CONTENTS

Thanks to my much missed nan, my parents, my sister, and my children, for being all I've ever needed and more. Love, laughter, and great genes. I was truly blessed.

Special thanks to Jim, for your continued support… and formatting skills. And to Skye for being my longest-serving internet BF – and provider of kindness in the form of flashdrives.

THE DOORWAY

Across the garden in your mind,
A hidden doorway you will find,
Open it and you will see,
A magic that will set you free.

Turn the handle, go on through,
Walk the ground stepped on by few.
With trusting eyes and bravest heart,
Watch the real world fall apart.

Colours rise into the air,
There's light and music everywhere,
Within it all, if you but look,
The dreams you had, the paths you
took.

An endless wood, a wishing well,
Enchanted beasts escaped from Hell.
All kinds of things within await,
For you to take a chance on fate.

Others will find that secret door,
But know not what they're looking for,
And some will bravely seize the day,
'Til truth insists they cannot stay.

But you are different, a dreamer born,
Your soul sees not with hate nor scorn.
Come sit with me, my writer friend,
Let magic flow until... 'The End'.

IMAGINATION

A beautiful creature, a promise just
born,
Yet, twisted, it takes you to its lair,
Guiding you, leading you, by the
hand,
Pulling you, dragging you, by the hair.

Kicking and screaming, you follow it
in,
As your soul becomes its willing feast.
Escape is an option you know you
should try,

As you recline there, chatting with the
beast.

Winding through dreams on glorious
wings,
Eternity seems but a passage in time.
Frozen, forgetful, and lost in the shade,
Should you remain, you'll drown in
sublime.

Extending your hand with a tentative
will,
You grasp at the edges, a little too late.
Swirling and tumbling, you fall at its
feet,
Smiling, eyes sparkling, you yield to
your fate.

FEMME FATALE

With bittersweet innocence,
And fragile inner grace,
Breaking hearts with every look,
She hides her real face.

Luring strangers into Hell,
They willingly comply,
Crashed and burnt on empty smiles,
The promise in the lie.

Beware the lonely angel,
She's never what she seems.
She'll make you wish you knew her,
Then haunt you in your dreams.

She'll take the passion from you,
Convince you it's to keep.
The danger will elude you,
She cuts you while you sleep.

When, at last, you understand,
The truth behind the lies,
You're half the man you used to be,
With a bullet between the eyes.

TIME

Time whistles past my window,
A fleeting thing, indeed.
It cares not for your pain,
It suffers not from greed.

Time whistles past my window,
On effervescent wings.
Although it offers hope,
No promises it brings.

Time whistles past my window,
I watch it, standing still,
Eroding as it goes,
It has the greater will.

Time whistles past my window,
And yet, I stare in awe,
Time is in the future,
And all that's gone before.

For time will wait for no man,
No man can hold back time.
I watch it whistle past,
And write its flight in rhyme.

MONSTER

"Did you miss me?" I ask.
He sits in his chair,
Eyes staring at figments,
That aren't really there.

He's gripping the armrests,
With such iron will,
His hands big and hairy,
Yet eerily still.

"Did you miss me?" I ask.
He speaks not a word.

His silence frustrates me,
I'm certain he heard.

He's frowning, eyes narrow,
That face I abhor.
But this time I'm braver,
Less scared than before.

"Did you miss me?" He'd ask,
At home every night.
And the answer I gave,
Had better be right.

I'm waiting before him,
The blows will not come.
The fear that I faced once,
Is finally done.

"Did you miss me?" I ask,
my hands wet and red.
I'm 'useless' and 'ugly',
But at least I'm not dead.

LADY OF THE THRALL

An eerie wind, unholy chill,
Grips the bones with iron will.
Deep amidst the deadened trees,
The lady falls onto her knees.

Enter here, if you be damned.
Her spell diverts from what you'd
planned.
With every step, her curse grows
strong.
Unto her world, you'll soon belong.

For she will send you raving mad,
With thoughts of guilt you've always had.
A torment made to match her own;
For fifteen years, it's all she's known.

There's no escape, no chance to flee.
Inside her wood you'll always be.
Madness sees your soul destroyed,
Lest of guilt you be devoid.

PAIN

I'm pain so hard, and deep, and true.
I'm all that life has put you through.
My presence fuels your darkest fears,
And echoes through forgotten years.

I'm everything you longed to lose,
The ones who tried to make you
choose.
I'm all the fury, all the grief,
The sin that turned you from belief.

Inside your mind, you look for me.
Yet shun the soul that calls to thee,
For I have taken all you knew,
The master thief revered by few.

Perhaps our paths were meant to cross,
For both of us encountered loss.
The shame, the guilt, the emptiness,
You had to know, you must confess.

I'm far from Hell, but yet I burn,
I'm it that means you'll never learn,
Eclipsing all that's pure and right,
Within my shade you hide from light.

And if you fear me, as you should,
I'll not depart, I never could.
We're one together, you and I,
For pain endures until we die.

THE BOOK

I came upon a man one day,
Who told me just to walk away.
He spurned my gaze and shed a tear,
And told of complex inner fear.

He wore a coat of brown and beige.
His boots and hair were grey from
age,
But in his hand he held a book,
Which gave me pause and made me
look.

The cover damaged, fading fast,
Yet clearly it was meant to last.
The spine was fraying, aged, and
worn.
The corners bent, the pages torn.

I asked the man what book he held.
I had to know, I was compelled.
He simply shrugged and looked at me,
Then raised the tome and bent his
knee.

With care I reached and grabbed the
book,
If just to take a closer look,
And as I did the man gave way.
He smiled and said he couldn't stay.

Then in a flash he fled that place,
A darkened patch left in the space.
With inner fear I stepped into,
The vacant shadow, and then I knew.

Decades past, I stood alone,
Afraid of that once kept unknown.
Then it occurred, so suddenly,
A person came and looked at me.

I told them, with conviction clear,
"Walk away. Do not come near."
But as I cried I saw them look,
Their eyes inquiring of my book.

WITHIN

Lost inside this rainy cave,
The water all around,
I contemplate the images,
Emerging from the sound.

Stalactites and stalagmites,
Formed from a million tears,
Figures flicker in and out,
With the passing of the years.

Sweet enemy, I know you're here,
With me, everywhere,
I need not see your silhouette,
I feel you when I stare.

And if you try to trick me,
With your cunning, desperate ruse,
There'll be no mind to con, you fool,
I've nothing left to lose.

So do your worst, you'll hear me say,
As I languish far below,
My laughter is a ricochet,
'Twill soon be all you know.

A KING'S REGRET

The old king sits upon his throne.
His eyes are pale, his sword is gone.
His silver armour's stained with rust.
His battle shield has turned to dust.

And yet he bares the wisdom old,
Of ancient lore and stories told.
Inside his heart a hero sleeps,
For youth, he neither pines nor weeps.

As shadows move around his hall,
He hears the battle trumpets call.
The clash of steel, the sound of death;
He'll hear it with his dying breath.

The scarlet stained the frozen ground,
As men were falling all around,
Amidst it all he felt no shame;
The old king cannot say the same.

With wisdom comes a cold remorse;
A bitter wind on death's pale horse.
He'll take his sorrow to the gates,
Where he will learn what fate awaits.

On mighty steed, in kingdom's name,
He fought and killed, and played the
game.
But time's an unforgiving foe.
It deals the lost their fatal blow.

Upon his throne, the old king rests.
No tears are shed, as he behests.
As darkness falls within his hall,
He answers one last battle call.

BEYOND FANTASY

Where dragons flew and giants trod,
Where kings and queens would lead,
Where knights on horseback proved
their worth,
There's nothing left but greed.

In forests deep and castles high,
'Cross waking chasms wide,
O'er craggy mountains capped with
snow,
What once was great has died.

The brave and strong of old are gone,
Their swords have turned to rust.
Majestic realms of elves and dwarves,
Are naught but earth and dust.

Beyond drear lands of modern day,
A world of wondrous light,
Is fading from our hearts and minds,
'Twill soon be far from sight.

The doorway to that magic place,
Is closing all too fast.
I fear the tales the bards did tell,
Were never meant to last.

I've seen the day that comes to us,
A time of death and war,
Of darkened days and broken lives,
Like none that's come before.

Where will we go when Hell's on earth,
To flee from fear and dread?
For the writers and the artisans,
Will all be cold and dead.

THE MISSING SELF

I met a man the other day,
He said his self had gone away.
I wondered then, what did he mean?
As he began to vent his spleen.

He looked at me with crazy eyes,
And told his tale with anguished sighs.
His self, he said, had left him there,
Abandoned, lost, it wasn't fair.

It left so quietly in the night,
No note, no kiss, no warning light,
And when he woke, next early morn,
He was alone, bereft, forlorn.

Still I stood and scratched my head,
Not comprehending what he said.
How could your self just leave you,
friend?
Were not you bonded till the end?

Alas, he said, we'd fallen out,
When last we spoke, did naught but,
shout
Bad words exchanged the night before,
I fear that's why he's here no more.

His woe retold he began to weep,
I could not watch him sink so deep,
And so I offered all I had,
My self was his, it made him glad.

Where I was going, I had no need,
Taking my self - no less than greed,
With hollow body I couldn't stay,
One last good deed, then I passed
away.

THE TORTURER

The man will come, you'll know not
when,
He'll crawl beneath your skin, and
then,
He'll smile at you with blood-drenched
lips,
Whilst sharpening deadly fingertips.

He'll taste your tears as he makes you sweat,
You'll beg to die, at least forget.
And when he's finally done with you,
He'll take his blade and run you through.

Alas, your tale will not end there,
For Hell is made of man's despair,
In fiery chasms, you'll languish on,
'Til time itself has been and gone.

Eternity of justice dealt,
Your skin will twist, and burn, and melt,
And when your soul can take no more,
He'll offer you an open door.

Yet if you take the path he shows,
Your soul be damned, that much he knows.
For every pain he put you through,
Peace only comes when you do it, too.

The souls he brings you scream and cry,
They beg you let them burn and die,
But as you look upon their sin,
Your soul grows hard, and you begin.

THE SOUL BEARER

With nimble fingers he loosens ties,
Releasing the soul as the body dies.
With muscular arms he takes the strain,
No mortal soul comes free of pain.

No backward glance, no parting stare,
He's toiled too long to linger there.
A hooded figure, he walks on by,
No mouth to frown, no eyes to cry.

For many moons he's done this task,
His shrouded face 'neath steely mask.
Each soul he takes might be his own,
The only one he's never known.

One-hundred-thousand years ago,
He lived as only rich men know.
A king of kings, a noble knight,
A warrior born to stand and fight.

But to his shame, he made a deal,
To feel as only poor men feel.
For just one night, he sold his soul,
His servant's wife his only goal.

With break of dawn the castle woke,
From noble men to common folk.
A shadow spread to claim the halls,
"The king is gone," rang out the calls.

Beside the woman still in his bed,
His golden crown and a note that read,
'One soul we take as payment just
For little more than sated lust.'

For now, the deathly plains he'll stride,
Where demons, ghouls, and monsters hide.
Six-feet tall and cloaked in black,
He holds the tide of evil back.

Saving souls from staying lost,
He will not fail, he knows the cost,
For if this curse he can endure,
One soul may be his only cure.

Hidden within an unknown name,
The demons played a spiteful game.
A kingly soul in body poor,
When death is nigh, it's moved once more.

One day they'll cease their cruel mirth,
His soul no longer to walk the earth,
And on that day he'll find release,
A cold, yet long awaited peace.

BITTERSWEET

Lovingly she whispers, silent and still,
Telling him secrets that no one else will,
Touching his skin after others have fled,
Controlling his soul from inside his head.

It's mercy she gives when mercy he needs,
Soothing his pain as he withers and

bleeds,
Holding his hand like the mother he lost,
Tranquil perfection concealing the cost.

A ravenous angel, shrouded and wrong,
Constant deception disguised in her song.
He plays his part well, a boy not a man,
There's no one to save him, nobody can.

He'll willingly linger, lost in quicksand,
He'll part with his life, all he loved, all he planned.
She burns like the sun and feeds his desire,
Secure in her arms, he yields to the fire.

THE TOWER

Beyond the darkened chasm,
Where nothing holy thrives,
There stands a stony prison,
Built from forgotten lives.

A tower made of evil,
One-hundred decades old.
Immortal souls its captives,
Their story never told.

The screams of those within,
Unheard by man and beast.
The governors hold the key.
Upon those souls they feast.

Trapped there in the dark,
With no eyes to look or see.
Each one can hear the voices,
Those with whom they long to be.

One-thousand years of anguish,
One-thousand years of pain,
One-thousand years of no reprieve,
They've long since gone insane.

By hope they've been abandoned,
As a flaming guardian stands.
But outside, in the distance,
A saviour crosses lands.

With magic in his blood,
Doomed race behind his eyes,
He'll bring the power of mage and
man,
To end the ancient lies.

He'll face the blackest magic,
And traverse the darkest lands,
To release a once great people,
From the false immortals' hands.

This poem tells in rhyme the story contained within my fantasy novel, The Sanctum of Souls.

A WANTED MAN

He tips his hat as he walks past,
His trigger finger twitching fast.
Fine leather boots on wind-whipped
soil,
His chaps and trench coat smoothed
with oil.

The metal gleams upon each hip,
Been that way since he left the ship.
His future owned by good lawmen,
Unsure he'll see his past again.

The scars are there for all to see,
The wounds he hides internally.
A wanted man, he took a deal,
Just one more life he'd have to steal.

To save his neck from hangman's
noose,
He'll find the one that he set loose.
Once a friend, a brother, his kin,
For clemency, he'll bring him in.

With guilt and grief his soul's
ensnared,
He lost the one for whom he cared.
Her heart, the bullet keenly found,
Not meant for her, she stood her
ground.

His mind remembers, pain runs deep,
He winces as he hears her weep.
His tears were dried 'fore being shed,
His vision turning vengeance red.

That night, his holster held his gun,
His brother fled, went on the run.
With shame he let him get away,
So he switched sides to make him pay.

Now he's returned; one last free ride.
They set him free, he knows they lied.
"Go bring him in", the lawmen said,
"Redemption comes when he is dead."

But wanted men do not go free,
No outlaw walks so easily.
And so, with borrowed badge and
gun,
He'll find him where the lawless run.

As kin, they'd both been first to draw.
But they're not brothers anymore.
A star on coat, no guarantee,
Another day this man would see.

He tips his hat as he walks past,
This cordial act may be his last.
But salvage from his own despair,
Be not the lawmen's to declare.

With borrowed gun, he'll find relief,
And though his triumph will be brief,
That man will see before he dies,
His old friend's hatred in his eyes.

ETERNAL LOVE

She lies in tattered robes of white.
Her satin skin untouched by light.
In dark repose, eternal grace;
I gaze upon my angel's face.

She loved me once, of that I'm sure,
But I will love her evermore.
Together bound by endless love,
Oblivious to the world above.

'Neath dirt and grass, and passers-by,
I hold her hand, say not to cry.
She is my breath, my better side.
No soul could say I hadn't tried.

To keep her safe, to keep her mine,
By fortune's hand, she'd sipped the
wine.
"Fear not," said I, as she did wake.
"My love is true, I'll not forsake."

She trembles as I dry her tears,
And swear my oath will last for years.
A lonely dawn she'll n'er receive.
With lasting passion, I'll never leave.

When last on moonlit ground we
stood,
She was not thinking as she should.
She was confused, I did not blame.
'Twas my desire that brought her
shame.

A mindless lapse, a man's weak will.
'Twas just a kiss, though hurt her still.
I had to show my heart was true,
So I set to craft a box of yew.

A lad was paid to shift the soil;
Sovereigns calmed his deep turmoil.
And in the time she sweetly slept,
I kissed her cheek and quietly wept.

Now awake, she clings to me.
Our hearts are joined for eternity.
"Hush my dear, it's over now,
Eternal love, my solemn vow."

ASSASSIN

A river washing over me,
My soul was lost eternally,
Swept away down rocky falls,
Too far to hear my voiceless calls.

A dagger clenched in leathered hand,
My choice at odds with what I'd
planned.
Too swiftly, life did take its leave;
No loved ones close to weep or grieve.

With blood on skin, and blood on
blade,
With one soul lost, and one in shade.
I'd never seen such silent eyes;
I closed them shut to hide their lies.

'A life must end', the missive read.
'Your payment due when she is dead'.
Yet as I looked upon the name,
I lost enjoyment of the game.

As I stood up, to step away,
I knew I'd lost my edge that day,
For even with a contract clear,
Her name I knew I'd always hear.

Her heart already known to me;
So long ago she set me free.
Another man soon filled my shoes,
But now her death was his to choose.

My heart left numb, I could not feel;
That place, my memories, so surreal.
In moonless night, I slipped away,
For what I'd done, no gold could pay.

A WRITER'S TALE

Stories flooding through my head,
Of knights, and elves, and mages.
Dragons roar with fiery breath,
My mind creates the pages.

"Let me in", my spirit begs,
Provoking revelation.
Edges blur and bleed within,
Divine imagination.

Tempting me from bleak-stained truth,
Are worlds for which I'm aching.
Magic thrives where dreams begin,
A wonder for the taking.

Roaming far away from fact,
For fiction yields more riches.
The pen is truly mightier,
When faced with beasts and witches.

From mere words a strength is found,
Where weakness once did dwell.
Heaven's light, just out of reach,
Grants sanctuary from Hell.

Eyes are closed and breath is held,
Waves crash upon a shore.
Fancy, broken free from binds,
Walks through the open door.

SWIFTLY COME THE SHADOWS

A reflection in a window,
As you wander quietly by.
A pin drop in the silence.
An echo of a sigh.

A single frozen teardrop.
A moment held mid-flow.
The passing of the years,
As the good times come and go.

Swiftly come the shadows,
And all that darkness brings.
Memories once eternal,
Now faded, pretty things.

Sleep well my fellow soul,
'Neath a sheet of pearly dust.
The earth will not forsake you,
For return to it you must.

THE DARK ONES

The dark ones come in dead of night,
To steal your dreams and hide your
sight.
With sharpened claws and taloned toes,
From where they venture, no one
knows.

With hateful glee, they bite and pinch.
They take your gladness, inch by inch.
Devouring all your thoughts and fears,
With eerie mirth, they sup your tears.

They sit on you, and with their weight,
They scorn, and mock, and burn, and
hate.
Invading all that's good and clean,
They torture, yet remain unseen.

They'll make you wake, alone, afraid.
The memory is slow to fade.
Return to sleep, a notion dread,
You lie there sweating in your bed.

Yet with the dawn, their power's gone.
You made it through, you will go on.
But still you'll hear them in your mind.
And know, come night, your dreams
they'll find.

LEGACY OF MAN

A creature lost to man's own greed,
For at his hands the earth doth bleed.
A single bullet changes all.
How many birds and beasts will fall?

The future is not ours to own,
Before we came the seeds were sown.
Upon this planet we must share,
We kill and take without a care.

But when we're done what will we leave?
A loss for future kin to grieve,
An empty space where beauty shone.
Will we not stop until it's gone?

How many lives must humans steal?
How can we teach the child to feel?
The magic held within the world,
At human hands will come unfurled.

Wolves and badgers, bears and boar,
Plus many hundreds gone before.
Plants and flowers, forests bold,
This earth we have in strangle hold.

We take its life, we take its soul,
Destruction seems our only goal,
And those of men who've seen earth's fate,
Do little more than watch and hate.

A day will come when we will see,
Our world's not as it ought to be.
But as men come to comprehend,
'Twill be too late to heal or mend.

On bland horizon we will stand,
To look upon a blood-stained land.
No fairer place we'll ever find,
For only earth could love mankind.

FAR FROM GRACE

Teardrops falling far from Grace,
As shadows wash across her face.
Pain entrenched inside her heart,
And heaven knows she's torn apart.

But the devil knows just why she cries,
As angels do not hear the lies.
Softly, bitter words cut deep,
Like blackened souls, they haunt her
sleep.

If only she could hear the voice
That left her life, 'twas not her choice,
For now she knows she's all alone,
Her crystal heart turned into stone.

Once laughter rang inside her ears,
She danced and sang for many years.
Then winter came and took to ground,
And something lost was never found.

Since then our Grace did lose her way,
She dragged her heels through every
day,
To contemplate a sweet release,
An emptiness that offers peace.

I watched our Grace before she left,
I'd never seen one that bereft,
For all I really wanted to,
I couldn't help, what could I do?

The shadows grew, they got stuck there,
They dulled her eyes, it wasn't fair,
To think of all she used to be,
That wasting lingers here with me.

Still, when she bade this world farewell,
I knew she'd found the path from Hell,
Her soul had left us long before,
And I know she smiled as she closed the door.

THE FAE

Betwixt, between
Their souls unseen
Above, below
They softly glow
Aside, astray
At break of day
About, around
Without a sound
Beloved, bejewelled
They'll not be fooled

Adept, adorned
They'll not be mourned
Hither here, hither there
On wings that sparkle in the air
Be they fae, be they not
Their time is n'er to be forgot
Of myth or truth
They cling to youth
Night or day
Or come what may
Through tome, through time
In ancient rhyme
A charm or curse
In voice and verse.

IT'S NOT GOODBYE

In heaven I will great you,
With words so long unsaid.
I'll remind you that I love you,
And stroke your furry head.
I'll bring your favourite toy,
The lead you left hung up.
I'll hold your furry paw,
And praise my well-trained pup.
We'll run 'cross sunset fields,
Together you and I.
Four legs in time with two,

Our bond will never die.
My heart broke into pieces,
The day you left my heel.
But your shadow's always been there,
I see, I hear, I feel.
My life will still go on,
We humans make it so.
But I know you'll be there waiting,
When it comes my time to go.

THICK SKIN

A thicker skin I need to grow,
But how I start, I do not know.
If there's an ointment in a vial,
That might just last me, for a while.

'Thick Skin for Dummies' - does that book exist,
On high up shelves I may have missed?
Do docs prescribe a special gel,
That makes your hide grow thick, as

well?

Do hardware stores stock special tools,
That twist and bend the skin growth
rules?
Or should I seek a magic route,
A witchy broth of eye of newt?

All that I know, is I must try,
To be thick skinned, not moan or cry.
And when next time, harsh words are
said,
I'll laugh, and dance, and bounce,
instead.

THE STORY OF THE SNOWMAN

Once upon a Christmas night,
When snowflakes fell in pale moonlight,
And footprints from some winter play,
Did fill with snow and fade away,
The brightest star up in the sky,
Looked down on earth and gave a sigh,
For from her seat in outer space,
She could not see a happy face.

In from the cold the children fled,
Tucked up inside each comfy bed.
The adults drew the curtains tight;
Each human face was out of sight.
And so she let her feelings show;
Straight down to earth there came a
glow.
Celestial beams, they touched the
ground,
As magic made a snowy mound.

Up and up the mound did rise,
Until it grew to human size.
Two fallen twigs some arms did make.
A life was formed from each
snowflake.
Throughout the night that star did toil,
Her creation cautious not to spoil.
The head and body nearly done,
Her time was lost, she felt the sun.

Soon to cast its warming ray;
A herald of a brand new day.
With scant time left to make it whole,
A carrot nose, two eyes of coal,
Were all she found in anxious haste,
Lest diligence be gone to waste.
But still she had to find a smile,
To make her effort all worthwhile.

Then as the light did reach the earth,
Some pebbles shone - restored her
mirth.
A perfect smile those stones did yield.
To dawn the snowman was revealed.
With spirits high, the star retired.
The snowman stood to be admired,
By children out for winter play.
How he arrived, they could not say.

But every single winter since,
With Christmas pud and pies of mince,
When lands lie 'neath white blankets deep,
Those men stand tall while children sleep
As curtains close, the star looks down.
She never sighs, nor wears a frown.
For from her grace came men of snow,
Made with love and magic glow.

FOR MY SON

When your day's confusing and your
mind can't take the noise.
When you're feeling like you're
different from the other girls and boys.
When you don't know why they
criticise, or tell you that you're bad.
When you ask for a little space, to stop
you feeling mad.

Just remember that I'm with you, and
you are not alone.
Please know I'll never judge you, never
leave you on your own.
If you put your trust in me, together
we will stand.
Let me guide you in this crazy world;
I'll take you by the hand.

I'll willingly watch over you, help you
see as others see.
I'll be there when you're feeling lost;
you can always count on me.
And when you're feeling down,
annoyed, misunderstood,
Just know I'll always listen; I'd change
things if I could.

When your little heart is aching. When
you think they pick on you.
When they tell you something's easy,
but it seems so hard to do.
When you simply cannot help, but lash
out at those around.
When you're feeling so ignored by
them, and yearning to be found.

When your head is on the table, and
you're shutting out the light.
When you cannot tell them why it's
hard, 'cause they always think they're
right.
When you simply want to run away,
so you're certain they aren't there.
When you wish they'd just be nicer,
and act as if they care.

Just remember that I'm here for you,
and you are not alone.
Please know I won't give up on you,
never leave you on your own.
Just put your hand in mine, my son,
and we'll be standing tall.
We'll walk together in this crazy world;
I'll catch you when you fall.

Written for my high-functioning autistic son as I watched him walk through troubling times.

DEMON

Tell me of thy hatred,
Tell me of thy lies,
Give me cause to smite thee,
I'll bring thee down to size.

With venom, speak thy wrath,
Thy righteousness be spake,
I'll give to thee a rope,
Enough to take and take.

Come sit here by my side,
Let not thy tongue be still,
I swear to treat thee fairly,
I vow to thee I will.

With fairness I shalt hear,
All the unkind words of thee,
And once thy rage is spent,
Thy fate I shalt decree.

For fifty-thousand years,
I've listened to such men,
Pride came before their fall,
It surely will again.

Some might call me 'demon',
As with evil, I reside,
But I am merely ears,
For the monster deep inside.

I'll be there in the darkness,
A witness to thy spite,
I'll hear thee, judgement free,
Then take what's mine by right.

Thy soul shalt not ascend,
The gates be closed to thee,
For my service to the gods,
Thy fate belongs to me.

THE LONG ROAD HOME

Travelling far from distant lands,
A winding trail of light.
No home is left behind them.
No will is left to fight.

Such sombre faces echoed,
Down the line of young and old.
As the hours changed to days,
Silent wanderers brave the cold.

Through mountain range and desert,
O'er plains of blackened stone,
Never turning to look backwards,
Lest the lost and burned be shown.

The spectre of displacement,
Weighs heavy on them all,
From mothers holding infants,
To warriors strong and tall.

And yet, a hope is present,
From the last man to the first,
Through their aching, bitter hunger,
And their barely sated thirst.

They strive to find a homeland,
As the wise men lead the way.
With slow procession onward,
They follow, come what may.

Their fears are cloaked in silence,
Concerns and doubts unsaid.
With the horrors far behind,
Lay the bodies of their dead.

No time was theirs to grieve,
As they fled their ruined lives,
Sisters losing brothers,
Husbands losing wives.

But amidst the devastation,
As flames seared flesh and wood,
Those that managed to escape,
Did not realise no one could.

Through a night that's now eternal,
Courageously they tread.
The souls of those once living,
Leave behind unburied dead.

A glorious home awaits them,
Of this, the wise are sure.
That winding trail of light,
Will find a home once more.

TREAD LIGHTLY ON THE ECHOES

Kiss me when I'm gone,
But do not linger there.
Listen for my name,
But remember not to care.

Keep your arms wide open,
But close your heart to me.
Follow the path we walked on,
But set your shadow free.

I'm a whisper in the wind,
A place where dreamers play.
I'd let you travel with me,
But I fear that you might stay.

Tread lightly on the echoes,
For they'll wake you from your sleep.
The future's waiting for you.
Your soul's not mine to keep.

There will be hands to take,
Even though they won't be mine.
If you let the magic in,
I promise you'll be fine.

Kiss me when I'm gone,
But make it just once more.
I'll be here when you're ready.
That's what Heaven's for.

LEGEND OF THE MUMMY

A woman once existed,
Embittered and embalmed,
As stiff and still as death itself,
Yet all the men she charmed.

A beauty of distinction,
She lured her lovers in.
With spicy scented sorcery,
She bade them leave their kin.

They came without regretting,
With minds already caught.
When close enough to smell their
souls,
She drew them in with thought.

Her bearing never changing,
Inflexible as stone.
But from within a fire burned,
The fiercest ever known.

With naught to give them pleasure,
No arms to make them stay,
No lips to tease or tantalise,
She had no other way.

Her need to really know them,
Had fuelled an era long.
As mortals leaned in close enough,
What once was there was gone.

For once there was a woman,
Resentful but at rest.
With all the men who came to her,
Absorbed into her breast.

The tales speak of her beauty,
With warning they do tell,
Of what lies 'neath her silken robes,
A passage straight to Hell.

SWALLOWS

One day quite long ago, a maiden stood ashore,
Held in loves embrace, 'fore he set sail once more.
She laid her head against his chest, not wanting to miss a beat.
He whispered, as he held her close, soon again that they would meet.

"When the stars are at their highest,
when the moon is full and bright,
You'll hear my voice, across the waves,
whisper your name each night.
I'll blow you kisses on the summer
breeze, caress you with the sun.
And when you see the swallows
return, my journey home's begun."

As his ship set sail that day, the
maiden's tears fell deep.
She held his picture to her breast, as
she cried herself to sleep.
Each night she prayed for his safe
return, and blew a kiss to sea.
Every day she watched the seasons
change, and waited patiently.

As the days grew long and lonely, and
the nights soon fell away,
She waited for the swallows; she
looked for them each day.
And as the winds blew warmer, and
the sun shone on her face,
She listened at the sea shore for the
waves to whisper 'Grace'.

Then the swallows soon returned, and
her soul felt light at last.
She sang herself to sleep each night,
her tears were in the past.
She knew that soon her love would be
by her side once more.
She couldn't wait to tell him what the
future held in store.

But soon the stars had lost some shine,
the moon hung low in the sky.
Grace still listened at the shore, but the
waves did only sigh.
No longer did she feel his kisses
blowing in the breeze,
And the warm fingers of the sun
slowly began to freeze.

As the news arrived with a scorn, that
his ship was lost at sea,
A dark cloud hovered there that day
and the rain fell endlessly.
The maiden's cries carried in the wind,
and the heavens felt her pain.
Never would she hold him close and
feel his heart again.

Though she remembered him most
always, each second of every day,
She couldn't quite remember, his
words as he went away.
All she could recall was the look of
love in his eyes,
The changing of the seasons, and the
urge to watch the skies.

Still many months did pass, and the
seasons changed once more
The maiden found herself waiting at a
place she'd been before.
As she held her baby in her arms, she
heard a whisper clear,
"Grace, I love you, I always will, and I
always will be near."

A tear rolled down her cheek, as she
felt a kiss in the air.
She smiled and turned her face to the
sun, as she knew that he was there.
She opened her eyes in time to see,
two swallows flying high.
She told her babe what daddy said, the
day he said goodbye.

"When the stars are at their highest,
when the moon is full and bright,
You'll hear my voice, across the waves,
whisper your name each night.
I'll blow you kisses on the summer
breeze, caress you with the sun,
And when you see the swallows
return, my journey home's begun.

GOODBYE, YOUTH

A girl in a courtyard, with tousled brown hair,
Laughs at the world like she hasn't a care.
She skips and she dances with a light in her eyes.
If I didn't know better, I'd say she fell from the skies.

She's open and innocent, unafraid to
be free.
Her heart's on her sleeve, and she's
smiling at me.
Does she know who I am, in this
fragile old skin?
So blissfully oblivious of the future
within.

From what I remember, it was me in
that yard,
Laughing and merry 'til time took me
off guard.
She can see me in the distance, though
she tries not to stare,
And as she skips down the road, she's
forgotten I'm there.

Goodbye, pretty girl with the tousled brown hair.
I hope you continue to not have a care.
Keep that light in your eyes for as long as you're able,
Leave that heart on your sleeve and your cards on the table.

THE DEMON'S CONSCIENCE

Within the darkest part,
Of your evil, twisted mind,
There's one who wears your skin,
A brother, of a kind.

He's you when you were born,
Before you touched the flame,
The innocence that fell,
When shadows stole your name.

He'd claw his way outside,
If you'd not cut his nails,
He sits there in the dark,
Immune to all your tales.

Of course, he sees your charm,
And knows why you delight,
But you he cannot stop,
You took his will to fight.

But each and every dusk,
As certain as the dawn,
You stand there face to face,
With he that you so scorn.

In dreams you can't avoid,
The angel in your shoes,
He'll talk until you vow,
He's nothing left to lose.

Through sleep you sense the man,
A burden in repose,
He calls to you and begs,
The only one that knows.

But eyes are simply screens,
Pulled up, he disappears,
With wickedness you smile,
Ignoring all his fears.

From within he watches,
Your fiery soul his cage,
Tormented by your mind,
With all its pain and rage.

There'll be no end for him,
Immortal as you be,
A prince of Heaven caught,
By your insanity.

ON BURNING FIELDS

We walked on burning fields,
Our footsteps drenched in death,
The smell of blood hung low,
We tried to hold our breath.

No Heaven touched those plains,
For Hell was all around,
The crimson of the sky,
Met bloodshed on the ground.

If ever there was peace,
It surely now was gone,
Obliterated lives,
The sight went on and on.

From east to west we walked,
From north to south we saw,
The echoes of the fight,
The torment, pain, and gore.

I took your hand in mine.
We searched amidst the lost,
But life blew scant on dust,
O'er burning plains we crossed.

And when we found the end,
Our hope all sucked away,
We turned and faced the truth,
Right there, we had to stay.

Two lovers in the sun,
The day the war came by,
We stood there holding hands,
We watched the arrows fly.

We walk these burning fields,
'Cross bodies drenched in pain,
Two spirits holding hands,
Forever we remain.

THE MOON QUEEN

The moon queen sleeps the day away,
Her fairer sister out to play.
As father time brings back the night,
His younger child comes into sight.

With hair of shadow and pale blue
eyes;
The beauty of the cloudless skies.
Yet few will look upon her face,
As she sets the moon into its place.

Unlike that which her sister wields,
A paler light her magic yields.
But in that light the earth is shown,
A thriving world by day unknown.

She watches as the owls take flight,
The field mice scamper through the
night.
The moths attracted by her glow,
The bats that spiral, swoop, and flow.

And as the month is drifting past,
Each phase is thinner than the last,
Until her light is barely there,
But still she lingers everywhere.

In the dark her soul holds sway,
Her influence not gone astray,
Because she knows that very soon,
The earth will once more see the
moon.

FAITH

Time's sweet sorrow, misty-eyed foe,
Endlessly soaring, but where will it go?
Hopeless avenger, of fair-weathered heart,
Tearing the satin-sheened fabric apart.

Onward and upward the mystics will cry,
Of battle they tire as they look to the sky.

"Take us" they shout to the creature they fear,
While demons grow fat on each scarlet tear.

No more will the haunted be lost to the song,
Shadows unyielding hold on to the throng.
Broken, so broken, blood-soaked and raw,
The eons have noticed what disciples ignore.

I came unto him with my soul-catching star,
I fell to my knees, and I watched from afar,
For I was the distance, the mile after mile,
And I could not reach, revere, or revile.

"Forever!" the knights, in their armour, did yell,
Then turned on their heels and merged with the swell.
The stories will tell of the foundling once lost,
But give no account of the terrible cost.

Forge onward my dear, forge iron and steel,
Take all that you can, for nothing is real,
Rest while you're able and learn what you must,
And always remember to trust the mistrust.

Wisdom is sown in the sharp sands of time,
Glory will find you in the word and the rhyme,
Bolster your strength with the lore of the west,
Fetter your valour 'til the moment is best.

The forgotten and desperate will cling to despair,
Too foot-sore to build, too brainwashed to care,
In their hour of darkness, you'll rise from the page,
History's scion set free from its cage .

LUMP

I have this thing inside of me,
It's somewhere that it shouldn't be.
A naughty thing, this little lump;
I'd like to give it one big thump.

It's sitting there, not doing much,
But splutters at the slightest touch.
I know it wants to grow some more,
But that's not what my body's for.

How dare it think that it can stay.
You stupid lump, just go away!
I will not stand for this intrusion.
No squatter's rights, just lump's
delusion.

Its time within me will be brief.
I'll brook no threat from lumpy thief.
Now don't get cocky, my bulgy
'friend',
There's just one way that this can end.

A lighthearted letter to my tumour, written back in 2014 after first being diagnosed with cervical cancer.

CALL TO ARMS

Shudder beneath the pulpit,
As your armour's stained with red.
Raise the mighty sword,
Left dormant at your bed.

Crucifix in hand,
You wield the strength of kings.
As tyrants sack your lands,
You cling to peace faith brings.

Holy and unholy,
Impaled upon past woes.
This temple fails to heal you,
As you yield to mortal blows.

In your heart, you lie defeated,
Cold blood runs 'neath your skin.
Yet still the battle beckons,
The darkness left within.

With furrowed brow, you linger,
Gods hand upon your chest.
But Heaven cannot save you,
As you're called to pass the test.

From the lectern you arise,
And the darkness bleeds the light.
Adorned in scarlet plate,
You heed the call to fight.

Your duty casts a shadow,
Over all you sought to be.
But choice is for the free man,
Not the king that dwells in thee.

SHADOWS

Some people live like shadows,
Barely seen and barely heard.
Quietly moving through trees of life,
Unnoticed, without a word.

They pass like whispers through
crowded rooms,
Displacing air, but nothing more.
Their footprints make no imprint
In the patterns on the floor.

They're the ones that walk right past
you
As you thought, 'is someone there?'
They're the disappearing colours,
They're the breeze that blew your hair.

They make so little impression,
That their presence is rarely sought.
They're the ones so seldom mentioned.
Never given a second thought.

They cry and no one comforts.
Their laughter is never shared.
They fall upon hard times,
Knowing no one really cared.

It's another dimension they travel,
One just slightly out of sync.
They may be glimpsed as they walk in,
Yet you'll miss them if you blink.

They barely rustle the leaves,
And their shadow is quickly passed.
With no echo in their wake,
The memories may not last.

One day they simply disappear,
With no moment to define.
With no one really noticing
Their departure or decline.

No stories told about their life.
No writing on the wall.
And the question remains unanswered,
Were they ever there at all?

MAERVELL

Above the darkened land below,
A kingdom sits in scarlet glow.
Once a place of endless mirth,
Now only shadows touch the earth.

As walls succumb to shades of green,
No words are heard, no face is seen.
The echoes of a bygone age,
Just fading words upon the page.

Silently the streets lie still,
No footfall comes nor ever will.
The halls of heroes sigh and groan,
No more their glory to be known.

Through broken glass, the ivy flows,
Round empty beds, it twines and
grows.
From kingly halls to common homes,
All life confined to dusty tomes.

The wind, unchallenged, wanders
there;
The cracks grow wide in disrepair.
Rainfall calls on unswept floors,
Invited in through broken doors.

And yet, amidst this vacant place,
Throughout the cold, forgotten space,
A memory whispers strangely clear,
Of elven folk of yesteryear.

A flash of colour between the leaves,
A trace of heat lifts to the eaves,
A child's delight, a melody,
A flicker of what used to be.

But whispers are not made to last;
What's done is done, what's past is
past.
At nature's will, the stone's reclaimed,
And absent souls are left unnamed.

Maervell exists within my fantasy novel, The Sanctum of Souls. This poem illustrates it perfectly.

DARKNESS

I am the darkest recess,
The corner where you hide.
I'm the secrets that you keep,
The bloody tears you cried.

I'm your screaming inner child,
That slumbers wrapped in fear.
I'm the one who answers for you,
When the real you isn't here.

I'm everything and nothing,
Bound up in all you've known.
I've been the key inside the lock,
The seeds of hate you've sown.

I am the one who haunts you;
'Neath morals I do dwell.
When your soul aspires to Heaven,
I'll drag you back to Hell.

You'll never cast me out,
However hard you try,
For darkness lurks in every man,
From birth until they die.

THE MOUSE AND THE MAGICIAN

Down stoney steps he scampered fast,
Afraid this night might be his last,
Until he came upon a door,
That barred his way across the floor.

He looked behind, his hair on end,
What followed him was not his friend.
A shadow grew upon the wall,
It must have been near ten-feet tall.

With fear he froze unto the spot,
His heart beat fast, his blood was hot,
And then he heard the dreaded sound,
As from the bend, the beast came round.

The candles flickered, the shadows stirred,
His heartbeat in his head he heard.
His time had come, he had no doubt.
He tried to squeal but naught came out.

From up above two eyes did glow,
Sharpened teeth sent fear below,
But as the fiend did make to spring,
A light enveloped everything.

Behind the prey the door was wide,
A taller shape stood just inside.
Up from the ground the victim rose,
And found himself faced with a nose.

"There you are, my dearest friend,
I feared that you had met your end.
Come with me, we'll put things right.
Let's cast just one more spell this
night."

Into the room the tall one paced.
The small one looked at what he'd
faced.
If he could smile, he would at that -
Disgruntled look upon the cat.

Once inside, the door shut tight,
The mouse took in the wondrous
sight.
A memory glinted in his mind,
But 'twas too big for furry kind.

All about the rounded room,
Were bottles, jars, a magic broom,
And at the centre of it all,
An altar stood, ornate and tall.

A swirling light of many hues,
Sparkling bursts of reds and blues,
Pops and cracks, a whirling hum,
He held on tightly to a thumb.

Further in his saviour went,
Until at last his walk was spent,
Gently setting down his charge,
Upon the altar, high and large.

The little one did start to dread,
Familiar thoughts ran through his
head.
The one who'd saved him from the
cat,
Had donned a cape and pointy hat.

Waving arms into the air,
The magic came from everywhere,
The air got thick, the words were weird,
The mouse did shake, 'twas as he'd feared.

Into the fire from frying pan.
He thought to run from magic man,
But as he tried to make a dash,
There came a loud and mighty crash.

A puff of smoke that made him blind,
The mouse could neither feel nor find,
His four short feet or tale so long,
It seemed his life had truly gone.

Yet soon the cloud was there no more,
The room still there, the walls the floor,
Though now not nearly quite as great,
What calamity had been his fate?

Confused, he sat upon the dais,
As memories came from many ways,
And when he finally found his feet,
A smiling face his eyes did meet.

"My friend, it seems you are returned,
How glad I am, and how I've learned.
Now, if you will permit me to,
I've one more spell that I can do."

That was all it took for mouse,
To run away and leave that house,
With longer legs and human will,
Of magic spells he'd had his fill.

On his way through door and hall,
He heard a noise that made him stall,
Away he sped o'er welcome mat,
Tucked 'neath his arm, a yowling cat.

SILENCE

There's silence here within my cell,
My cold and undeserving Hell.
A scratch, a scamper, at my feet;
At least there's something left to eat.

They went away some time ago.
Quite why they left I do not know.
The voices in the corridor,
Grew anxious, then were heard no
more.

I sit and listen to the sound,
Of nothingness that's all around.
I've naught to do but contemplate,
The sands of time, the twists of fate.

I wonder if they will return;
I'm sure that I smell something burn.
Ah well, I'll have to wait and see,
Endure this silence, patiently.

TAINTED LOVE

Meet me in the sapling wood,
The sun might shine there, if we're
good.
Our hearts might dwell as one,
entwined,
A glory long, a love maligned.

They say we're fools to think such
things,
Our love was forged on devil's wings.
They came and took our lives away,
But they were right, or so they say.

I loved you then, my dearest heart,
No words could tear our souls apart.
We shared a life, we shared a birth,
By blood we came to mother earth.

Alas, our bond was loathed by all.
We roused their wrath, we had to fall.
With twisted minds, they saw our fate.
The deed was fuelled by fear and hate.

As one we came unto their place.
As one we burned, without a trace.
But souls not judged by mortal law,
Are free to love for evermore.

Meet me in the sapling wood,
No one will question if we should.
For there, we'll not be judged by men,
Amongst the trees, we'll live again.

THE LAST DRAGON

In time's long sleep
The dragon sings
Of mythic dreams
Eternal things
Of endless truth
Enduring might
Enchantment binds
The longest night
Beneath the skin
Of steely scales
The beast recalls

Forgotten tales
The fire cooled
The wings grown still
Unnatural rest
A warlock's will
In magic chains
The giant's bound
A captive soul
Beneath the ground
In cavern deep
Where none do dwell
His keeper casts
The darkest spell
From netherworlds
The magic came
It bled his soul
And called his name
An ancient force
A banished mage
With sorcery
He fed his rage
And thus he spake
With blackened verse

The warlock falling
To his curse
Through him he quelled
A legend great
The creature's breath
Could change his fate
And so the dragon
Lingers on
His wings are tied
His spirit gone
For while he draws
Eternal breath
The mage escapes
Infernal death
The warlock and
His charge secure
Enslaved, entrapped
For evermore.

A PRAYER FOR MY CHILDREN

Keep them safe, o Lord above, and
watch their little souls.
Help them lead productive lives, and
realise all their goals.
Fill their little hearts with love. Free
their minds from the weight of pain.
Lift them higher when life pulls them
down; give them the strength to rise
up again.

Touch them with your faith, o Lord,
and help them see through the night.
Bestow upon them the power to smile,
and laugh with all of their might.
Please keep my children safe, o Lord. I
pray you their lives not to take.
May they see the dawn of many new
days. Bless the imprints their footsteps
will make.
Forgive the sins of their mother, o
Lord; don't let them take after me.
Give them the courage to follow their
dreams; make life all that they want it
to be.
And when their time on this earth is
done, please give them the peace they
are due.
And guide their souls back to heaven,
and let me be waiting there, too.

Let me dance with them in the
sunlight. Let me sing them to sleep
'neath the moon.
Let me enjoy them as much as I'm
able, lest it all be over too soon.

DEAD SHEPHERDS

They walk in darkened days,
When hunger comes to call.
The whispers on the wind,
Bring fear to one and all.

When cold has found a way,
Into the souls of men.
The bonds of hearth and home,
Will turn to dust again.

They'll walk and they will wait,
Dead shepherds at your door,
To claim the wretched flock,
Of those who walked before.

In every age of man,
When sunlight takes its leave,
A reckoning will come,
And all who live will grieve.

From darkness there's no flight,
No place in which to hide.
You’d best be sure you know,
They'll find their way inside.

And if you can escape,
Be sparing with your ease,
As time can taint the pure,
Bring saints to sinner's knees.

THE TREACLE'S ARSE

Down in the valley where the
misanthropes grow,
There lived a young treacle whose
name I don't know,
With hair made of sunshine and eyes
crystal clear,
And a beautiful chain that stretched ear
to ear.

In his coat made of blueness and his boots brown as muck,
He sang of the good times and he gave not a fuck,
He leapt and pranced and he woke all the dead,
With the ungodly shrillness that rang from his head.

Now old mother Grimstone, she knew what he sought,
For he'd told her his tale when her cakes he had bought,
As he scattered the crumbles to the east and the west,
He looked to her bosom and pronounced his behest.

"Old Stimgroan," he said with his face full of trite,
"I need you to make me a wrong that is right,
For in all of my years putting goodness to seed,
I've yet to encounter a bad people need."

A bad people need? Now this vexed mother's mind,
She'd n'er heard such tripe, so she smacked his behind,
"Oh thank ye" he cried, as he grabbed at his arse,
His bottom stung much, but his misery was sparse.

His eyes ringing gleeful, he opened his
maw,
And to all but the skeevalls the music
was pure,
All vale folk were drawn to the
glorious song,
As that dear little treacle found a right
come from wrong.

Now, I know only little as I was
absent that morn,
But it seems that our friend had long
been forlorn,
A gidget had stuck in his throat as he'd
chewed,
For treacles are well known for wolfing
their food.

For moons he'd been singing his sunrise refrain,
Through the holes of a gidget, he'd brought only pain,
As old mother Grimstone had wacked his round bot,
The blockage burst forth, an incredible shot.

To this day I hear him, that strange little thing,
Putting bad things to good with songs left to sing,
His riddle unriddled with a slap and a shriek,
Happy as fluff, though he couldn't sit for a week.

THE END

At nature's feet I sat a while,
Amidst sweet grass and chamomile.
At her behest, I lingered long,
And felt the void when she was gone.

So true was she, the purest grace,
The sunshine on such wholesome face.
A testament to time's great will,
Yet time on earth does not stand still.

The shadows fell and dulled the
flowers,
As I endured her closing hours.
Her pity came and went, it seemed,
I wept alone as darkness dreamed.

With deep remorse, sincerest woe,
I pulled the shadows to and fro,
Until, at last, a light was found,
Amidst green shards upon the ground.

A tiny seed, a wondrous bliss,
No mortal mind imagined this.
A gift my lady left to me,
Of earth and air, and land and sea.

I could not aim to just restore,
The many wonders sown before.
But hope it sings a rousing verse,
And burns away the darkest curse.

The Doorway and other poems

ABOUT THE AUTHOR

R.K. Pavia was born in Winchester, England in 1976. She now lives in Lincolnshire, in the same, quiet village in which she grew up from the age of ten. She shares her life with the three most special people in it – her children.

A self-confessed 'weirdo', she has a variety of interests, including music, history, psychology, philosophy, and serial killers.

When she's not writing she's playing video games, chatting to her mum, or ranting at politicians on the television.

Also by R.K. Pavia

The Sanctum of Souls: Book One of The Gadrionis Chronicles (debut fantasy novel)

Published as Bex Pavia

The Dark Ones: A Collection of Rhyming Poetry (audiobook)
The Story of the Snowman (an illustrated children's book)

To get in contact and for more information –

mageguildpublishing@outlook.com

www.facebook.com/RKPavia

https://twitter.com/RKPavia

https://writingsofaweirdo.wordpress.com

www.ingramcontent.com/pod-product-compliance
Lightning Source LLC
Chambersburg PA
CBHW070629030426
42337CB00020B/3960